D0470896

The Spirit of
IRELAND

Text
Paul Nolan

Commissioning
Andrew Preston

Design
Philip Clucas

Editorial
David Gibbon

Photography
Colour Library Books Ltd
The Bord Fáilte
Michael Diggin
Tony Ruta
John Hinde Ltd

Photo Research
Miriam Sharland

Production
Ruth Arthur
Sally Connolly
Neil Randles

Director of Production
Gerald Hughes

© 1993 Colour Library Books Ltd
All rights reserved
ISBN 1 85833 074 2

The Spirit of
IRELAND

Paul Nolan

A JOHN HINDE PRODUCT

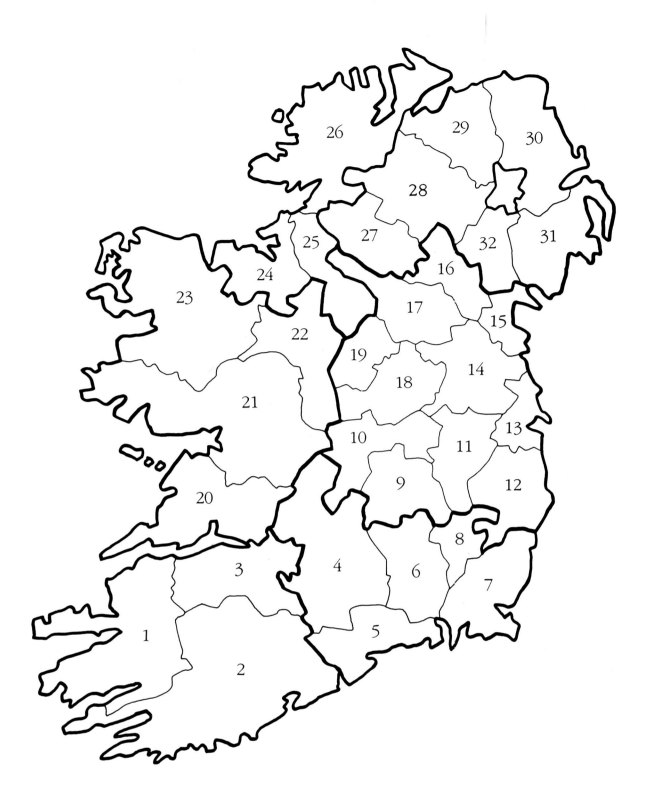

THE SOUTHWEST	EAST AND MIDLANDS	THE WEST	THE NORTHEAST
1 KERRY	9 LAOIS	20 CLARE	27 FERMANAGH
2 CORK	10 OFFALY	21 GALWAY	28 TYRONE
3 LIMERICK	11 KILDARE	22 ROSCOMMON	29 LONDONDERRY
	12 WICKLOW	23 MAYO	30 ANTRIM
	13 DUBLIN		31 DOWN
THE SOUTHEAST	14 MEATH		32 ARMAGH
4 TIPPERARY	15 LOUTH	THE NORTHWEST	
5 WATERFORD	16 MONAGHAN	24 SLIGO	
6 KILKENNY	17 CAVAN	25 LEITRIM	
7 WEXFORD	18 WEST MEATH	26 DONEGAL	
8 CARLOW	19 LONGFORD		

CONTENTS

Sybil Head on the Dingle Peninsula, County Kerry.

If there is a land on earth dominated more by the heart than the intellect it is Ireland. The beating pulse of that ancient heart is to be found on an empty windswept hill standing above the valley of the River Boyne. The Hill of Tara stands between three worlds. It is very much a solid and substantial physical presence in today's world of reality. Its prehistoric past takes it back to the period before Christianity came to Ireland, when this was the seat of the High Kings of all Ireland. And Tara reaches into a third world, the world of legends, where ancient gods and heroes pursue their age-old feuds and loves, breathing the spirit into modern Ireland. When Daniel O'Connor led his movement against British rule in the 19th century he came to Tara. About one million people gathered to hear him speak here in 1845.

Today Tara is an impressive grass-covered hill, the smooth crown of which is dotted with the monuments from its great past. These earthworks date back at least 4,000 years and show Tara to have been a site of great importance for many generations. The oldest of the monuments is a huge tomb which contained around 100 bodies, known as the Mound of the Hostages. One body, that of a teenage boy, was buried with magnificent jewellery. Clearly, even then Tara was the home of noblemen and heroes.

As with so much about Tara, the Mound of Hostages stands on the border land between legend, history and modern science. Its name derives from a well-known legend concerning King Cormac Mac Art, the great lawgiver. During one of the many wars of his reign King Cormac took hostages, whom he imprisoned in a hall. When his enemies broke their word Cormac caused the hostages to be killed. Romantic historians have linked the legend of the hostages to the ancient burial mound on Tara.

North of the Mound of the Hostages is the Banqueting Hall, a vast sunken depression some 750 feet long and 90 feet wide. It is named after the great feasting hall of the Fianna, the warrior band that served King Cormac Mac Art. Here the fighters, poets, historians and noblemen gathered to celebrate the great pagan festival of Samhain, in the autumn. Early texts describe the magnificent ceremonial and ritual division of foods and the never-ending flow of beer. The feasts of Samhain were great and orgiastic affairs filled with drunken laughter. Unfortunately for such romantic views, the Banqueting Hall is almost certainly a thousand years too old to have been the home of Samhain feasting in the court of Cormac. It was probably a sunken processional way leading to the summit of the hill.

Other earthworks, such as the House of the Kings, Tomb of Tea and Fort of Loiguire Mac Neill are similarly misnamed. Undoubtedly there were fortified palaces, feasting halls and pagan sanctuaries on Tara, but the purpose of those earthworks which remain had little to do with their modern titles.

Only the most mystic of all survives under its original name. This is the sacred stone, the Lia Fail or Stone of Destiny. This provided the climax of the crowning ceremony of the High Kings. The man wishing to claim the honour of being High King had to clamber on top of the stone. If the holy stone roared its approval three times the new High King was deemed to have been accepted by the gods. In Christian times this pagan stone was given a veneer of respectability by the claim that it was the stone which Jacob had used as a pillow. Today the stone is carved with the inscription '1798 RIP' in memory of those Irishmen who died in the rebellion of that year.

King Cormac Mac Art himself is known from many legends and histories written down between the ninth and 12th centuries, and much of Tara's mystery is linked to his name. In legend he was the High King who ruled all of Ireland from Tara and had at his command the mighty Fianna, a warrior elite of 20,000 men under the leadership of the hero Fionn. Cormac was said to be 'wise, learned, valiant and mild, not given causelessly to be bloody as were his ancestors.' He ruled all of Ireland and the lands of the Irish Scots, now Galloway in Scotland. He died as the result of a Druid's curse, by choking on a salmon bone.

Historically there is only scanty evidence for either Cormac or Fionn in the third century. Some of what there is hints at conflict with the Romans in Britain. It is likely that there was a High King in Tara at this time, though how far his power extended is unclear. Nor is it entirely certain whether the power of the High King was secular or mystical and religious. But, whatever the truth of the High Kings of Tara, they remain real in the national makeup of the Irish. It has always been to Tara that the Irish look for national identity.

From Tara it is possible to see much that is typical of Ireland. The view of rich pastureland and neatly edged fields stretches out across the eastern counties, speaking of the great agricultural wealth which has long been the basis of the Irish economy. The ruined earthworks hint at the heroic Celtic past now submerged beneath a Christian present.

The land which the Irish inhabit is without doubt one of the most splendid in the world. It has been said that visitors come to Ireland for the scenery, but leave remembering its people. It is certainly the scenery, with its promises of tranquil beauty and rich salmon fishing, which draws strangers to Ireland for vacations. But once they arrive, travellers find Ireland a magical land, with charming and welcoming people only too happy to make their stay a rewarding and memorable experience.

The island of Ireland is varied in both landscape and character, but in general conforms to a pattern. Much of the interior is made up of a vast limestone plateau drained by the River Shannon, which flows southwards to enter the Atlantic Ocean below Limerick. Around the edges are the hills and mountains which make the coastline so dramatic and impressive. The hill of Tara itself stands where the high coastal mountains descend to lower, rounded hills to the north of Dublin.

The fertile hills stretch inland along the valleys of the Boyne and the Blackwater to the Bog of Allen and Lough Ramor. Largely composed of rocks and gravels left behind by retreating Ice Age glaciers, these hills are small and steep, unlike those elsewhere. Within the productive valleys are nestled some of the oldest and most historic of Ireland's monuments.

Admiring the view during a walk over the eastern hills.

Downstream from Tara is the great tomb of Newgrange. Constructed about 2,500 BC, Newgrange displays the mastery of architecture which Ireland can boast even at this early date. It is the finest of the ancient tombs known as passage graves – the Mound of Hostages at Tara is another – and is unique in many ways. Like all passage graves, Newgrange consists of a circular mound enclosing a central burial chamber approached by a long passage. It stands some 30 feet tall and is over 10 times that in diameter. Surrounded by a circle of standing stones and enclosed by a wall of glittering white quartz, the mound is dramatic in the extreme. But most enigmatic of all is the spectacular event which happens each year on the 21st December. On that day, and that day alone, the rising sun sends its light straight down the entrance passage to bathe the burial chamber in a rosy glow. Within minutes the cunningly constructed passage shuts off the light and the interior is plunged back into its usual darkness. The imagination of the design and the skill of the builders is amazing, dating as the tomb does from about the same period as the Egyptian pyramids.

Further downstream from Newgrange stand two bloody sites. The first is the ford where the Battle of the Boyne was fought in 1690 between the ousted Catholic King James II and his Protestant successor, King William III. William won the battle and James fled to France, leaving Ireland to his enemy. More brutal still was the fate which overtook the city of Drogheda near the mouth of the Boyne. In 1649 Oliver Cromwell arrived to deal with the Royalist Catholics in Ireland who had massacred Protestant settlers and threatened the hold of the Puritanical Republicans in England. After a siege of just nine days Cromwell broke into Drogheda and killed around 4,000 soldiers and citizens. He lost just 64 men himself. Such ruthless action soon quashed his enemies and Cromwell sailed home to London.

Today, Drogheda is a charming shopping centre and port serving the surrounding countryside. Most of the finest buildings date from the 18th and 19th centuries and include private mansions, civic buildings and pubs.

Further north, beyond Dundalk, is the wild and romantic Cooley Peninsula. The mountains and hills of Cooley are a ramblers' paradise. The heather covered hills offer endless miles of footpaths passing through some of the most magnificent scenery in eastern Ireland. These hills are largely untouched by modern life and unfold to the eye at a gentle and unhurried pace. Until only a few years ago Gaelic was the language of everyday life, but English has now taken over for most purposes.

The Cooley Peninsula is the setting for one of the greatest legends of pre-Christian Ireland: The Cattle Raid of Cooley. Medb, Queen of Connaught, led her army east to steal the Brown Bull of Ulster, which lived in Cooley. As the Ulstermen were sick with a magical sleep only the hero Cuchulainn, the legendary Hound of Ulster, came to face the Connaught army. The lengthy and beautifully crafted tale follows the heroic and brutal exploits of Cuchulainn as he delays the army of Medb long enough for the men of Ulster to recover from the magical curse.

This legendary cycle belongs to an earlier period than that of Cormac and Fionn. Cuchulainn fights with weapons and chariots typical of the period before Christ. His world is one of magic and enchantment. Gods and goddesses mix easily with humans, playing their part in the extraordinary and complex cycle of tales which carries Cuchulainn from his birth as son of the god Lugh to his death at the hands of a druid and a magical spear.

On the heather-covered slopes of Cooley it is easy to slip back in imagination to the violent, vibrant and exciting world between reality and myth where Cuchulainn galloped in his chariot and sang his war songs.

From the heights of Cooley can be seen perhaps the most beautiful, and certainly the most famous, mountains of Ireland. The Mountains of Mourne have been celebrated in song and poem, but the physical presence is more powerful than anything written. From a distance the heather-coated bulk seems almost gentle, with smooth slopes and soft silhouette. But anyone who has climbed in the Mountains of Mourne will know that within the smooth outlines seen from afar lurk tough granite crags and precipitous slopes which try even the most experienced fellwalker.

The Mourne Mountains are made up of ancient granites, but are relatively new as mountains go. The tough stone of which they are composed has long formed the basis of a flourishing local economy. The stone is quarried in quantity for building works in the nearby towns. Though the slopes themselves are covered by only thin soils, the valleys shelter fertile fields where traditional farming communities still exist, and the coast is dotted with superb harbours, home to numerous fishing craft which reap the rich harvest of the Irish Sea.

Some miles north of the Mountains of Mourne the narrow River Slaney winds inland. In AD 432 a storm forced a small ship to put into the Slaney for shelter. On board was a Christian missionary destined to sweep away the pagan Ireland of Cuchulainn and Fionn. His name was Patrick, and he had earlier been a slave in Ireland before escaping to France. Landing on the banks of the Slaney, Patrick met the local king Dichu. The pagan lord was at once converted to the new faith and gave Patrick a barn in which to live. The town of Saul derives its name from the Gaelic for barn, and it was here that St Patrick began his mission to convert the wild Irish to Christianity.

St Patrick travelled extensively throughout Ireland over the years, preaching the gospel to all who would listen. He even visited the Hill of Tara to confront the pagan priests on their own ground. There, Patrick met Laoghaire, High King of Ireland. Though the saint failed to convert the great king, he was allowed to preach throughout his realm. The fact that St Patrick preached mainly in Ulster and Connaught may reflect the extent of the secular power wielded by the High Kings at this time.

Many stories are told about St Patrick and his mission. The tale of how he used the three-lobed shamrock to explain the concept of the Holy Trinity is well known, but perhaps the most dramatic is that of the Easter Fire. On the pagan festival which coincided with Easter it was customary to put out every fire in the land. All of Ireland was plunged into darkness for the night until new flames were kindled at a special ceremony. But St Patrick kept a bright fire blazing on a hilltop in full view of the pagan priests. Those who have been in remote countryside, far from street lights, on a dark night, will know just how bright a distant light can appear. Patrick's holy fire must have created a stir indeed.

But wherever he travelled, Patrick always returned to be near his first convert. Just south of Saul was a massive hill crowned by an immensely strong fortress, the Dun Cealtchair. Now the city of Down, this crag became a central focus for early Christianity. There have been a succession of churches and abbeys on the hill, the present cathedral dating back only a century. A large granite slab beside the tower marks the spot where, locals claim, St Patrick is buried along with St Brigid and St Columba.

Many believe this claim to be spurious, the invention of a 12th century Norman adventurer, John de Courcey. The real burial place of St Patrick, it is argued, is on an equally impressive hill, that of Armagh. It was here that St Patrick established his cathedral, and with good reason. He and his faith had been welcomed by the King of Ulster. Only a few years earlier the great Navan Fort, military base of the Red Branch warriors of Ulster, had been destroyed by the forces of the High King of Tara. The royal family was sheltering on the Hill of Armagh, and St Patrick felt it wise to build his church on the easily-defended hill.

Armagh quickly became the religious centre of Christian Ireland. Scholars and clerics flocked to the hill to continue the learning and holiness established by St Patrick. While much of western Europe plunged into the darkness of barbarism, Armagh continued to show the light of civilisation. The great age of this centre of learning only came to an end with persistent and violent Viking raids in the 9th and 10th centuries.

Little now remains of the ancient Armagh, but it retains its holy reputation. This, combined with the seven hills of the city, have earned it the title of 'The Irish Rome'. There are now two great cathedrals in Armagh, the oldest being that of the Protestant Church of Ireland, which stands on the site of St Patrick's original. On a neighbouring hill stands the more elaborate 19th century Catholic cathedral.

North of Armagh spread the open waters of Lough Neagh, Ireland's largest lake. Legend states that the giant Finn Mac Cumaill, sometimes known as MacCool, created the lough when he tore a handful of earth from the spot and hurled it eastwards to form the Isle of Man. Though the lake makes for excellent fishing, especially for eels, it is not popular with tourists, for the shores are bleak and marshy and there is little in the way of scenic beauty on offer.

Very different are the hills to the north; the famed Nine Glens of Antrim. These romantic glens are beautiful to behold, but not easy to reach. The rugged mountain scenery ensured that the glens remained cut off from much of Ireland until the modern road was driven along the coast in the 19th century. Until then the area had been more closely tied to the sea and so to Scotland. For many years this region was ruled by the MacDonnell clan, the Lords of the Isles. A branch of this ancient family now holds the Earldom of Antrim.

A deserted country cottage, one of the better, 19th-century rural homes.

Though the coast road has made the Nine Glens more accessible, public transport is still limited and the secluded villages remain somewhat isolated, particularly in winter. This is an area where traditional culture remains strong. Some is revived in the summer specifically for tourists, but other aspects of music and dance are a natural part of everyday life.

Just north of the Nine Glens lies perhaps the most famous feature of Ireland's coast, the Giant's Causeway. Legend ascribes this to the same Finn Mac Cumaill who created Lough Neagh. It is said that Finn had an argument with a Scottish giant who lived on Skye, a magical island which was home to many legendary figures. Finn gathered together a vast number of stone stakes, which he drove into the sea bed to create a causeway across to Skye. Arriving there he was tricked into believing the Scottish giant was larger than himself. Retiring quickly to Ireland, Finn tore up his causeway, leaving only the stumps which now remain.

Science, however, has it that the causeway was created when massive outpourings of basalt welled up from deep within the earth and spread out to form deep beds of rock. As these cooled they formed large crystals with regular shapes, the polygonal columns of today. Subsequent erosion by wave and wind has worn away the surrounding rocks and shattered the basalt to leave the Giant's Causeway as we see it now.

The far northeast of Ireland is occupied by County Donegal, a land with a reputation for independence and a culture quite different from the rest of Ireland. It is a reputation which has been well earned and dates back centuries.

At the neck of the wild Inishowen Peninsula stands the abandoned fortress of Grianan of Aileach. St Patrick came here to preach, and conversions were made. Most important of the converts was Eoghan Ui Niall, son the semi-legendary Neil of the Nine Hostages and founder of the great O'Neil clan which dominated Ulster for centuries. At this time Grianan was already nearly 2,000 years old, having begun as a neolithic ritual centre. In 1101 the O'Donells of Tyrconnell, distant cousins of the O'Neils, sacked Grianan. It has been a ruin ever since.

West of the Inishowen Peninsula Donegal begins in earnest. The western mountains are spectacular in the extreme. The Derryveagh Mountains, in particular, are the haunt of ramblers,while Muckish and Errigal are the most often climbed, offering gentle slopes and magnificent views. Nestled between the sweeping uplands is the oddly named Poisoned Glen. The origins of this name are unclear, for the water here is no less palatable than in other uplands streams and loughs.

The wilder regions of Donegal are among the most staunch Gaeltach, or regions speaking Gaelic for everyday use. But here the Gaelic is notoriously different, being a dialect more akin to Hebridean Gaelic than to the official Irish language based on the tongue of Leinster. The traditional life of the mountain people of Donegal has much in common with that of the Scots across the sea. Like Harris, and other Hebridean islands, Donegal is famous for its tweed cloth, the sheep which graze the windswept uplands providing the wool for this warm and weather-resistant material.

Marking the southwest of the County of Donegal is Donegal town and Donegal Bay. The town is a bustling and vibrant place with numerous shops, restaurants and bars surrounding the central market place, known as the Diamond. In the centre of this open square is a monument to the Four Masters, brothers who wrote a history of Ireland in the 1620s. The book which they produced, *The Annals of the Four Masters*, contains much of the history and folklore of Celtic Ireland just as that society was changing beyond recognition with increased contact with England.

Interaction with the English led to some of the most pitiful tragedies of this area of western Ireland. In 1588 the storm-scattered ships of the Spanish Armada were desperately clawing their way home after a severe mauling by English ships in the Channel. Many vessels, battered by guns and winds, made for western Ireland. There they hoped to find shelter from the storm and help from the Irish. The Spanish believed the Catholic Irish would help their co-religionists against the Protestant English. They were to be bitterly disappointed.

All along the coast from Donegal south to Kerry the Spanish came ashore. Many ships were wrecked on the treacherous shoals and rocks off the beaches. One man counted over 1,200 corpses washed ashore on a single beach. Those who did land met a hostile reception. The English feared the Spanish were the vanguard of an invasion and shot those they met. The Irish, meanwhile, gleefully pillaged the survivors. Shipwrecked men were robbed of money, jewellery and even the clothes they stood up in by the Irish peasants they thought were their friends. Nobody knows how many thousands perished on the western coast.

The harsh western shores where so many lost their lives in misery and disappointment have changed little since the grim events of 1588. The towering cliffs still stare out across stormy seas crashing on treacherously-hidden rocks and shoals. And nowhere are the coasts more dramatic than in the three great western counties of Galway, Mayo and Sligo.

Sligo is the most northerly of the three. Its coastline is low, but it hides numerous shoals which were uncharted and dangerous when the Spanish ships sought shelter here in vain. Behind the coast rise the massive Slieve Gamph, the Ox Mountains. This vast expanse of unpopulated upland is carpeted by bogs and heather to the exclusion of almost everything else. Largely unattractive to walkers, the mountains are saved by the dramatic bulk of Benbulbin.

Rumoured locally to have been a fortress of Fionn and his Fianna warriors, Benbulbin is an isolated mountain rising to about 1,700 feet above sea level. Its flat top and sheer walls make it a striking feature. The upper parts of the rock are composed of tough limestone underlaid by soft shale. As the shale has eroded, the limestone has remained largely intact, giving rise to cliffs and gullies of dramatic aspect. It is said that the great warrior Diarmuid, who had once saved Fionn's life, was killed by a boar on the slopes of Benbulbin. Diarmuid had earlier stolen Fionn's wife, and though Fionn could have saved Diarmuid he refused to do so.

Further south the high ground runs right into the sea, forming impressive cliffs and a coastline rugged in the extreme. Inland the landscape takes on an aspect typical of western

Ireland. Open stretches of thin moorland grass interspersed with bogs and outcrops of bare rock are encountered here. In places mountains rear up out of the generally flat landscape, but bogs are the rule.

In the far southeast of Mayo is the town of Knock, the greatest pilgrim centre in Ireland. In 1879 a vision of the Blessed Virgin, St Joseph and St John appeared one evening about dusk on the gable wall of the parish church. Though it was raining heavily, the wall remained dry as long as the vision lasted. This was at once counted a miracle by local people and the church at Knock became a centre of pilgrimage.

In 1976 a new church was constructed to help cope with over half a million visitors each year. Ten years later a new airport was opened at Charlestown, and this has not only helped the pilgrims but has opened up most of western Ireland to tourists.

Overlooking the famous Galway Bay is the wide-spreading County Galway. The most famous part of the county is Connemara, the western portion of which pushes rocky headlands into the Atlantic. Like Mayo, this is a land of bogs, heaths and mountains. Farmland is hard to come by, and is generally worked with traditional methods and with age old tools. The Connemara is possibly the most visited and popular region of western Ireland for tourists, combining, as it does, all the old charm and wild beauty of the Ireland of popular imagination.

Just offshore lie the Aran Islands, famous for their woollen jumpers. These were traditionally knitted out of unbleached wool into thick garments for the fishermen who put out from these rocky islands. Each family had its own distinctive pattern, so that in the event of a tragedy the bodies of drowned sailors could be more easily recognised. Today most Aran sweaters are mass produced for the tourists, tourism being one of the main industries of the islands. The islanders are fluent in English for the benefit of outsiders, but tend to speak their own Gaelic when alone.

These western counties form the heart of the ancient kingdom of Connaught, the home of Queen Medb, who led the cattle raid on Cooley and faced the hero Cuchulainn. The fortress of Connaught which links the legendary to the historical in much the same way as does Tara, is the Cruachan in Roscommon. This rambling site was first inhabited in about 600 BC and was probably abandoned by AD 800, though a lack of archaeological excavation makes any statements open to doubt.

According to legend Cruachan was the centre of power in ancient Connaught. Medb, nicknamed 'the Drunken', ruled here with great ferocity and greater splendour. It was Medb who launched the wild warriors of Connaught into war against Ulster. How much truth there is in these legends is uncertain. What is known is that the Ulstermen and Connaughtmen were traditional enemies at the dawn of history. The Ui Neill dynasty which tore Ulster from the grip of its native rulers were probably the descendants of a Connaught royal family. At about this time massive earthworks were built along the borderlands between the two provinces. Dated to about AD 100, these fortifications faced south, as if the Ulstermen were on the defensive before the ferocity of Connaught.

South of Galway Bay, made famous in song, lies County Clare. Like the three western counties north of Galway Bay, Clare formed the western bastion of the kingdom of Queen Medb, but later became free and eventually passed into the Province of Munster, which covers southwestern Ireland.

Clare is a musical county in a musical country, and traditional dances are still performed enthusiastically. The people of a village will gather for small local dances, while larger events with famous bands will draw dancers from a wide area. Much of the music played is the traditional folk music of western Ireland. Quite unlike the sentimental ballads popular among the emigrant Irish, this music is concerned with the day-to-day realities of life in a farming community on the edge of the European culture.

Clare is a well-defined county. To the west is the Atlantic, to the north Galway Bay, to the south the Shannon Estuary and to the west the Shannon itself. Within these boundaries Clare is remarkably diverse. The southern lowlands are made up of rich and productive farmland spread around the county capital of Ennis.

In the north the weird landscape of The Burren seems as though from another planet. This great plateau of limestone covers around 75 square miles (200 square kilometres) of Clare. The rock lies bare and exposed for acres at a stretch, though the numerous cracks and crevices sprout

A boat among the reeds of Lough Gill near Castlegregory, County Kerry.

grass and wildflowers in profusion. Numerous underground rivers have carved caverns beneath the bare Burren rocks, and the most famous of these are at Aillwee, where the long-dried course of an underground river is today decorated with stalagmites, stalactites and other weird rock formations.

The thin soil of the Burren is poor for farming but harbours a magnificent collection of wild flora. Northern winds have brought south seeds of Arctic plants which flourish among the rocks. Similarly, the seeds of Mediterranean plants have been brought to the Burren and have found the virtually frost-free climate much to their liking. In this highly-individual habitat local species have flourished and diversified into a unique collection of plants. Botanists from all over the world come to study the curious flora of this area.

The fabulous scenery of The Burren is echoed in the dramatic coastline of western Clare. Mile after mile of towering cliffs and isolated stacks line the shoreline. The far point of Clare is at Loop Head, where a huge stack rises to the full height of the cliff, leaving a yawning chasm 30 feet wide. It is said that the Ulster hero Cuchulainn leapt this gap to escape a witch. The name Loop Head, is an anglicised version of the Gaelic words meaning 'The place of the leap'.

It was from the wild but fertile lands of southern Clare that the greatest of all Irish kings, Brian Boru, emerged. King of the small Dal Cais tribe which inhabited the bogs north of the Shannon estuary, Brian Boru was initially a relatively unimportant ruler. But he was determined to change all that.

Using the bogs and forests of Clare to good advantage, Brian began a guerrilla war against the wealthy Viking settlers in Limerick. A chronicler wrote 'However small the injury he might be able to do, Brian preferred it to peace.' At times Brian was reduced to leading a raiding party of just 15 men, but his determination and skill at acquiring plunder at little risk made him a greatly respected leader in Clare. At the age of just 26 Brian announced that he was going to attack and plunder the city of Limerick itself. Dal Cais messengers rode out across all of Clare and neighbouring counties calling warriors to follow Brian Boru. Numerous men flocked to join him, including the greatest freelance raider of Munster, together with his personal warband of 100 heavily armed men.

Brian Boru met the Viking army on the plain beside Limerick. Battle was joined at dawn, and until noon the two armies continued to hack at each other. Then the Vikings broke and fled to the safety of the city. But no safety was to be found, for the Irish poured in, slaughtering everyone who offered resistance, raping the women and enslaving everyone they could capture alive. The city was looted of its contents and then burned to the ground.

With this victory behind him, Brian could count on the support of all the kings of Munster, so long as he continued to give them success in battle and plunder in victory. In AD 1000 Brian marched against Leinster, defeating and looting Irish and Viking alike on the way, to take the rich prize of Dublin. Two years later he marched on Tara itself. He unceremoniously removed King Mael Sechnaill mac Domnall from the hilltop palaces and proclaimed himself High King of Ireland. None of the northern Irish warlords felt inclined to challenge King Brian and he enjoyed several years of peaceful rule.

In 1013 the men of Leinster and the Vikings rebelled. Ulster and most of Connaught refused to help Brian put down the revolt, so in 1014 he faced the gathered hosts of Vikings from Orkney and Denmark at Clontarf with only his Dal Cais and Munstermen warriors. In the savage fighting the Vikings and Leinstermen were heavily defeated, but Brian was killed, as was his mighty son Murchad. The High Kingship passed to Brian's son Tonchad and grandson Tairrdelbach, but neither were of Brian's stature. The brief glory which had come to County Clare as home to the High Kings of Ireland vanished as that position passed to the Kings of Connaught.

Limerick, the city which Brian sacked with such savagery, is today the third largest town in the Republic of Ireland. It is a major industrial centre, though unemployment has been high in recent years. It owes much of its importance to its position. Although its name is derived from the Gaelic for 'The Barren Place', Limerick is well placed for trade. The city stands at the head of the Shannon Estuary, and it has been said that anyone travelling through Ireland will end up in Limerick. It was its position which brought the Vikings to found the town and to which it owes its continuing prosperity.

Beyond the city itself County Limerick is a rich and fertile county dotted with prosperous villages and small towns relying on the agricultural produce of the land. Dairy produce is a major industry in Limerick, as is horse breeding; indeed, the horses of Limerick have long been famous as courageous hunters and reliable mounts. The landscape is dotted by ancient ruins. Not only are there numerous raths and prehistoric fortresses, but Norman castles and medieval monasteries are also encountered throughout the county.

Limerick is, however, best known for its style of light-hearted poetry. So characteristic are the five-line verses that they have taken the name of this county and are known everywhere as 'limericks'. The poems originated as a form of drinking wit much enjoyed by the locals, who would invent short verses about local characters. Often a group would construct a whole series of verses about each other as the whiskey bottle emptied of an evening.

Some of the poems with a more than local appeal were translated into English in the 1840s by James Mangan, who carefully retained the familiar beat which gave the poems their popularity. They were an instant success in England and America. Soon limericks became a standard vehicle for satire, humour and nonsense. Their popularity has never diminished, and limericks remain the best known feature of Limerick.

Also best known for its literary connections is Tipperary, the focus of a famous World War I marching song. It is easy to see why the hearts of so many were, according to the song, still in Tipperary, for it is one of the most gently beautiful of Irish counties, with the lush pastures and rich farmland of the aptly-named Golden Vale. But the most outstanding feature of Tipperary are its two dramatic hills: Slievenamon and Cashel.

Rising to over 2,300 feet (700 metres), Slievenamon is the taller of the two and is distinguished by its nearly conical shape. This is said to have been the fortress of King Bodb of the mythical warrior people Tuatha de Danann, and more recently to be the home of magical and entrancing fairy women. The great hero Fionn came to Slievenamon and spent many happy days dallying with the fairy women. Deciding at last to marry, Fionn chose Grainne, the beautiful daughter of King Cormac. Fionn knew he could not afford to anger the fairies so he declared that he would marry the first to run to the top of Slievenamon, having already told Grainne to hide herself on the mountain top. Thus Fionn got the bride he wanted without angering the powerful otherworld maidens.

Though much lower, the Rock of Cashel is more important historically. The easily-defended limestone crag has been fortified since prehistoric times and was the main fortress of the Kings of Munster when Tara was the seat of the High Kings. In 450 St Patrick baptised King Aengus on the rock, and in 977 Brian Boru came here to take the title of King of Munster. By the 12th century the rock was a religious centre, and most of the remains visible today date from this period. The only secular building left is the dramatic Round Tower which formed a centre of defence. The 12th century cathedral was heavily restored in the 17th century, though the tiny Cormac's Chapel remains largely untouched.

If Limerick and Tipperary are known through verse and song, Kerry is famous through jokes. Just as Americans tell jokes about unsophisticated Poles being foolish in the cities, and the British tell jokes about the Irish in general, the Irish tell jokes about the Kerrymen. In popular culture the Kerryman is daft, though not necessarily stupid, and entirely unversed in the sophisticated ways of town life, making him easy prey for tricksters and jokers alike. In truth the Kerrymen gained this reputation through their rural culture, but there is little backward about the county.

Daniel O'Connell, the greatest Irish leader of the 19th century, was born at Cahirciveen in Kerry in 1875. As a lawyer and politician O'Connell strove to improve the conditions of the Irish Catholics. In 1826 he founded the Order of Liberators, which won many freedoms. In 1829 Catholics became entitled to sit in the British Parliament, and O'Connell was elected for County Clare the next year. He won many valuable concessions of practical benefit for the Irish in Westminster, but as he grew older he became unable to control his more headstrong and violent younger colleagues. He died in 1847 leaving a divided and embittered movement.

Nor have the Kerry people been at all backward in exploiting the magnificent scenery of their county for their own benefit, and tourists are welcomed here with open arms and a vast array of creature comforts. It is impossible to travel far in Kerry without coming across souvenir shops, restaurants, cafes, pubs, hotels, camping grounds, bed and breakfast farms or any of a dozen variations, each of which affords the visitor comfort, while the astute Kerry residents get the cash.

The two great visitor attractions in Kerry are the Dingle Peninsula and the Ring of Kerry.

The latter is the more popular, being a scenic drive around the Iveragh Peninsula which runs for 110 miles (180 kilometres) and can be comfortably completed in a day. The magnificent coastal scenery of the Ring of Kerry is considered the loveliest feature, and rightly so. Dotted along the road are numerous other places to visit, including the ancestral home of Daniel O'Connell, as well as prehistoric remains.

The Dingle Peninsula is both smaller and more charming than the Ring of Kerry. There are numerous monastic remains and ruins scattered among the mountains and hills of Dingle together with raths and fortresses of an earlier era. On a mountain outside Kilmalkedar stands the shrine of St Brendan. It was here that the 6th century monk had his vision of the Hy-Brasil, or Islands of the Blessed, which sent him on his voyages in the Atlantic. The story of his journeys were written down years later and consist of accounts of trips to known places, such as the Orkneys and Iceland, together with unknown lands which some historians have identified as Florida or the Caribbean islands. The name St Brendan gave to his holy islands lives on in the country of Brazil.

For the tourist more interested in food than historical romance, Dingle has a fine reputation as a centre for seafood, and few of its restaurants will disappoint the lover of fine fish.

Off the far tip of Dingle lie the Blasket Islands, which have been uninhabited since 1953, when the last islander left for a more congenial life on the mainland. For many years before the final abandonment of the Blaskets, the young people had been leaving to seek employment in the cities and abroad. Such a drift has been typical of Ireland for generations, but on the Blaskets it was particularly strong and led to a declining population and a fading of the old ways.

The traditional life of the Blaskets has now gone, but it is recorded in numerous books and poems, for these tiny islands were unusually rich in culture. It was a life dominated by the sea in all its moods, and by the eternal westerly winds bringing rain and mist off the Atlantic. Today the Blaskets may be visited by ferry during the summer, though the crossing is notoriously difficult and the sea may change in minutes from flat calm to impassable waves. If the weather closes down the visitor has a choice of accommodation on the islands, but only in the summer, for winter finds the islands left to the seabirds and seals.

If Kerry is the county of peninsulas and wild coastal scenery, Cork rivals it for the title, and the two counties are famous for their rivalries. But Cork is not only a county of majestic coastlines; it is the largest county in Ireland and so one of the most diverse.

The southwest is indeed a place of dramatic coastlines, with Mizen Head, Sheep's Head and Dursey Island reaching far out into the grey Atlantic Ocean. The northern coasts are as wild and rugged as anything in Galway or Kerry, though further south softer red sandstone cliffs create profiles equally steep, but somehow gentler and less rugged.

On Mizen Head a lighthouse stands a short distance from the cliffs, linked to the shore by a frail suspension bridge across which lighthouse keepers must walk to take their post. The Sheep's Head is far more remote, being virtually cut off from public transport and approached by only a lonely and narrow road. Beara Peninsula, the most northerly of the three Cork headlands, runs along the north shore of Bantry Bay, a notoriously treacherous stretch of water.

Inland the landscape is one of upland moors and bogs interspersed by mountain peaks. These are particularly impressive in the west, though the east has its charm. The most famous stone in Ireland lies in eastern Cork, at Blarney. The stone is set into the battlements of the impressive Blarney Castle, and it is said that those who kiss it gain the power of flattering and persuasive speech, the proverbial 'gift of the gab'. Unfortunately for those tempted to gain this useful power, the only way to kiss the stone is to dangle upside down from the battlements while someone hangs on to your ankles to prevent you from falling to your death on the rocks below. More than one brave heart has quailed at the thought of the attempt.

It is said that the stone received its magical properties from Dermot McCarthy, Lord of Blarney, who ruled this region during the 16th century. When English messengers arrived from Queen Elizabeth demanding tribute and action against Catholic rebels, Dermot McCarthy promised everything he was asked for, but did nothing. Elizabeth sent new messengers, but Dermot put them off with fair words and lavish banquets. Every time the English came to Blarney the story was the same. They were given endless promises, magnificent entertainment, but never any solid results. Eventually, when yet another mission returned to London with promises from McCarthy, Elizabeth is said to have grinned ruefully. 'What he says he does not mean,' she said.

'It is the usual Blarney.' The word quickly entered the English language and this little village acquired fame and fortune.

As the coastline moves east it becomes progressively lower and less dramatic, though equally charming. By the time Waterford is reached it has become almost tame. There are a few cliffs where the low hills reach the sea, but in general Waterford's shoreline is one of open bays, sweeping beaches and gentle contours. It was to this coast that St Declan came in the early 5th century. The fact that he arrived some years before St Patrick has been well established, but his activities seem to have been mainly local, so St Patrick retains his reputation as being the man who converted Ireland.

At Ardmore can be seen the ruins of the monastery St Declan founded when he arrived here. The remains seen today date back no further than the 7th century, with the most impressive buildings being of later medieval date. The tomb of the saint may also be seen.

Waterford City itself stands near the head of the sheltered sweep of Waterford Harbour, by the spot where the three counties of Kilkenny, Wexford and Waterford come together. The town is best known for its crystal ware, which is exported worldwide. But the crystal is a relatively new product, having its origins in a factory founded in 1783. Waterford has been a major trading centre for over a thousand years. The Vikings founded this city, giving it the name of Vadrafjord, from which the modern name is derived. The Norsemen retained control of the city until the Norman adventurer Richard de Clare, nicknamed Strongbow, took it. Under whichever master the city has flourished, it has remained a wealthy trading centre quite distinct from the fertile farming lands around it. While cosmopolitan Waterford city established early links with Europe and other nations, the countryside remained virtually unaffected. Even today isolated Gaelic-speaking villages are to be found.

The counties of Kilkenny and Wexford join with Carlow to form a distinct region of Ireland which is quite unlike the rest of the island in many important ways. This is the only extensive lowland region south of Ulster where the rivers drain eastwards into the Irish Sea, rather than south along the Shannon or west direct to the Atlantic. The Barrow, Nore and Slaney drain the uplands which fringe the inland boundaries of these counties. Those same uplands prevent the prevailing wet westerly winds reaching the region with quite the effect that they strike elsewhere. The southeast is the driest and warmest region of Ireland. Many of the coastal towns are holiday resorts, much frequented by Dubliners.

Culturally, too, this region has its own characteristics. In part this is no doubt due to the long connection between these counties and Wales and England, not far across the St George's Channel. As the Roman Empire was breaking up Irish pirates took the opportunity to raid western parts of Britain. In many regions these raids took on the aspect of colonisation. Commemorative stones engraved with Irish Ogham script are found scattered throughout Wales and the West Country. The Irish colonists were eventually expelled or slaughtered by Cunedda, a northern British warlord, and his sons, in a war which lasted from about 430 to around 500.

In 1068 the MacMurraghs of Wexford led an army to Bristol, but failed to capture the city. A century later Dermot MacMurragh took the fatal step of employing Anglo-Norman mercenaries in his war against the men of Waterford. Over the following years large numbers of Normans, English and Welsh came over, both as warriors and as settlers. This region rapidly became partly Welsh in character, with strong English undertones in a basically Irish culture. Contact across the sea remained strong, with trading links and family connections continuing for centuries. It was therefore something of a shock when this region flared into revolt in 1798 with an intensity not seen elsewhere. It took the English several weeks and a full scale campaign to put down the rebellion. The climax came at Vinegar Hill, where battle raged for 12 hours before the peasants were overwhelmed with much slaughter.

A typical glimpse of the rich history of the region is captured in Kilkenny City, where solid reminders of the past are to be seen and visited. Originally a monastic settlement, Kilkenny experienced the full range of the power struggles that swept across Ireland. In 1169 the Norman adventurer Strongbow arrived and built a castle beside the town. Originally a rough timber outpost, the castle has been rebuilt and improved many times since. Today it is a powerful stone presence which towers majestically over the city. Most of the buildings to be seen today were restored or rebuilt in the 19th century with a touch of the medieval grandeur to which great barons such as Strongbow aspired.

A shepherd on the high grassland of the Dingle Peninsula.

Rather more of the medieval fabric is left in St Canice's Cathedral, which stands at the far end of Kilkenny from the castle. Named for the 6th century monk who founded the first monastery here, the cathedral is largely 13th century in date. This is possibly the purest medieval cathedral in all Ireland, and the numerous tombs within trace the rise and fall of powerful families with grim reality.

Not far from Kilkenny is one of the most famous monasteries in Ireland. Kells sits amid sweeping green fields beside the Kings River in the lush Kilkenny countryside. The massive surrounding walls testify to the need for defence in this, the most fertile of Ireland's regions. Within the towers and bastions stands a tumbled church which even in ruin is an awesome sight. With its dramatic arches and fine carving, Kells can still show us how fine the buildings must have been before they fell into decay.

As the coast moves north it leaves behind the sheltered and fertile lowlands of Kilkenny to rise towards the bleak mountains of Wicklow. Historically this area marked the edge of the Pale, that area around Dublin which the King of England could securely call his own during the medieval period. The Wicklow Mountains were home to the formidable O'Tooles, nominally subjects of the MacMurragh kings of Leinster but in reality fiercely independent. The O'Tooles retained their freedom until the end of the 16th century, when Wicklow finally became part of the Pale.

When rebellion flared across Ireland in 1798, the men of Wicklow rose with alacrity under the command of one Michael Dwyer. Numerous battles and ambushes followed, but in the Wicklow Mountains the rebellion was carried out with unusual compassion. Dwyer forbade the killing of civilians or ill treatment of captives. Even looting was kept to a surprisingly low level. When Dwyer was captured by the English his style of fighting earned him escape from the noose. Instead he was transported to Australia, where he went on to make a successful and respectable civic career.

The mountains where Dwyer and the O'Tooles lived and fought their wars of raid and counter-raid are among the most dramatic in eastern Ireland. Though not tall, the peaks are windswept and bare of any plants save the ubiquitous heather. The famous Wicklow Way, a signposted, long-distance walk, winds through this spectacular countryside and is popular with the citizens of Dublin, who can reach it in less than an hour. The path follows roads as little as possible and in places descends to sheep tracks barely wide enough to tread. It is a romantic and wild walk, but one to be treated with caution. Like all the rugged parts of Ireland the Wicklow Mountains are treacherous and dangerous.

When the potato famine depopulated Ireland in the 1840s, Wicklow suffered less severely than elsewhere, though the number of inhabitants fell from 125,000 to 100,000. The misery prompted a local Protestant landowner, Charles Stewart Parnell, to take up the cause of Irish home rule and land reform. In 1886 he gained the Tenant's Relief Bill, which eased many of the land problems. But in 1890 he was named as co-respondent in a sensational society divorce scandal and his career collapsed in ruins. Nevertheless, he had gained a great deal for Ireland and his house at Avondale is kept as a museum to this man who changed things for the better.

Inland of the Wicklow Mountains the ground falls gently in rolling hills to the upper reaches of the River Liffey. The slopes finally peter out onto the plain known as The Curragh. Famous for the staying power of its horses, The Curragh is the centre of the Irish horse-breeding industry. The National Stud lies outside Kildare and is a magnificent example of how a stud should be run. The only odd features are the astrological decorations and the glassed roofs of the stalls, which allow the stars to shine directly on the horses within. Founded by Colonel William Walker, a keen amateur astrologer, in 1900 the stud passed to the British Royal Family before becoming national property in 1943.

Not far away is the Curragh racecourse, where the classics of the Irish racing season take place. The Irish Derby, 1,000 Guineas and the Irish Oaks are all run over these beautiful, sweeping grasslands. It has been said that every Irishman is a born horseman, and on The Curragh it is possible to believe that.

Further down the Liffey stands the great city of Dublin, and here too the horse heritage remains strong. Many children and youngsters keep ponies on the rough stretches of grass which intersperse the city sprawl. For those accustomed to cities which hold only neatly trimmed parks and no animal larger than a dog, the horses of Dublin are something of a surprise. There can be no doubting the passion of the horse owners, nor the care they lavish on their mounts, and races and competitions are taken very seriously.

One Sunday each month the horse-owning community gathers on Smithfield for the greatest horse fair in western Europe. Farmers and travellers converge on Dublin to trade and gossip about horses. This surprisingly rural pastime in a capital city may be explained by the fact that Dublin has grown enormously in the past 30 years as vast numbers of people moved in from the country.

Dublin is a strange city, full of charm and attraction but with its full share of run down splendour and indifference. When archaeologists discovered the remains of the 9th century Viking settlement which founded Dublin, the Dubliners built a concrete office block on top of them, while many of the magnificent Georgian mansions of the city have been subdivided into tiny flats and allowed to fall into disrepair.

Despite these unattractive features Dublin remains a great city. It was founded by Vikings and became the capital of the Anglo-Norman adventurers who came to Ireland in the early medieval period. The greatest of these fighters, Richard de Clare, known as Strongbow, is buried in the Christchurch Cathedral, which he built in 1172. Dublin remained the chief city of Ireland and the centre of administration throughout the period of British rule. During the later 18th century wealthy landowners gathered in Dublin, where they built large and luxurious houses for themselves. The Dublin Season came to rival the London Season for fashion and elegance. It is to this period that many of the city's finest buildings belong. Unfortunately, several were destroyed by 19th century rioting and the Easter Rising of 1916. The gaps have been filled by more modern buildings.

But the chief charm of the city is without doubt its people, which is apt in a nation such as Ireland. Among famous Dubliners of the past are Oscar Wilde, the Duke of Wellington, Dean Jonathan Swift, James Joyce, George Bernard Shaw and Samuel Beckett. Today the city is a bustling hive of activity. O'Connell Street is the widest city street in Europe and is decorated with numerous statues, cafes and shops. Nearby are Moore Street and Henry Street with their markets. Many pubs and bars specialise in music and singing, an activity open to all with a voice and knowledge of traditional songs. The theatre district, which spreads across both sides of the Liffey is famous for the quality of its work. Traditional plays and musicals jostle with avant garde works and plays in Gaelic. There is never any reason to be bored in Dublin.

It has been said that Ireland is a nation ruled by the heart, and nowhere is that more true than in this jewel on the Liffey. For a capital city Dublin is remarkably local in character. The Irish are affectionate towards, rather than proud of Dublin, and, as with Ireland in general, there is a lot to be affectionate about.

THE

SOUTHWEST

Mountains frame this view of one of the many loughs to be found on the Ring of Kerry, a 110-mile, scenic drive.

Three of the inhabitants of the Blasket Islands, County Kerry, who live on the islands only during the summer.

The popular gardens of Muckross House, which attract many visitors with their famed rhododendrons and azaleas.

A horse enjoys a snack, while the driver of the trap slakes his thirst in a nearby inn.

Early morning crowds gather for the July Killarney Races, County Kerry, which attract thousands of people.

The peaks of MacGilly-cuddy's Reeks, the highest mountains in Ireland, loom behind Inch Beach.

The steps on the bleak island of Skellig Michael, County Kerry, which lead from the landing stage to the ruined, 6th-century monastery.

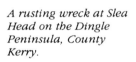

One of the dry-stone
monk's cells of St
Finian's Abbey, on
Skellig Michael. The
Abbey was sacked by
Vikings in 823, but
refounded soon after.

The cluster of six beehive
cells which stand beside
a holy spring on Skellig
Michael. It was here that
Olaf Trygveson, first
Christian king of
Norway, was baptised.

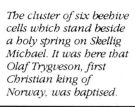

A rusting wreck at Slea
Head on the Dingle
Peninsula, County
Kerry.

A weaver, one of several traditional craftsmen at work on the Muckross Estate.

A small herd of cattle being driven along one of the more remote lanes of rural Kerry.

A typically rugged coastal scene from County Kerry, with sparse, sheep-grazing countryside.

A quiet drink in one of the many Gaelic-speaking bars in rural Kerry.

The much-patched trousers of a farm worker, photographed near the beautiful market town of Tralee.

Cottages scattered across the rich grazing land which surrounds Killorglin, County Kerry, a town renowned for its cattle fair.

A shepherd in Kenmare, a town famous for its knitted garments, tweed cloth and rugs, all made from local wool.

A small lobster boat upturned for routine maintainance on a beach, on the Dingle Peninsula of County Kerry.

The view from this wayside cross looks out across the deserted Blasket Islands at sunset. The last native islanders abandoned their ancestral homes in 1953.

The colourfully dressed Wren Boys who parade annually through Dingle, County Kerry, a rare survival of the rituals of medieval peasants.

Horse trading at the Puck Fair in Killorglin, originally a goat fair which is thought to date back over 2,000 years.

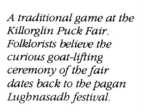

A traditional game at the Killorglin Puck Fair. Folklorists believe the curious goat-lifting ceremony of the fair dates back to the pagan Lughnasadh festival.

Brightly painted cottages display the individualistic taste of villagers in the Eyeries of County Cork.

Dursey Island sheep, famous for their tough, weather-resistant wool, are penned in, ready for shearing.

Fully equipped to stave off thirst on a chill spring day, a villager waits outside the pub at Nad, County Cork.

The statue of the Virgin Mary at Ballinaspittle, which is said to move miraculously by itself on certain nights, and which attracts large numbers of pilgrims.

A market stall in Cork, filled with locally produced goose eggs and plucked geese.

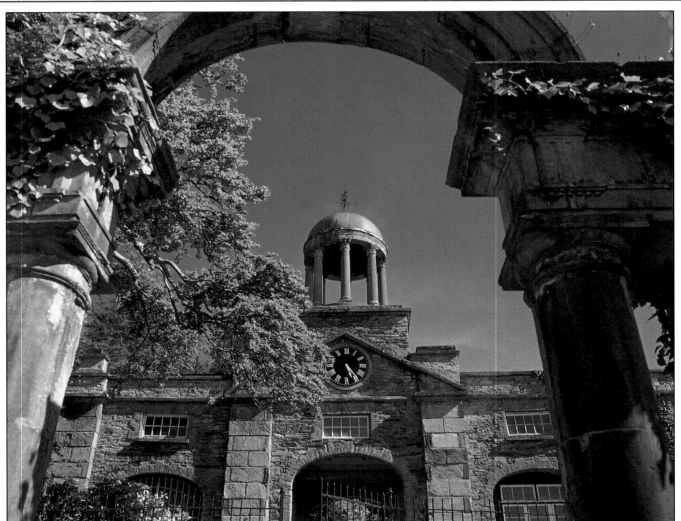

The fine, mid-18th century Bantry House is still lived in by descendants of its builder, and is currently undergoing lengthy restoration work.

The rich and fertile lowlands of County Cork, an area famous for its trout fishing.

Paddy Bourke's Bar on Cape Clear Island, County Cork, is situated near the birth site and church of St Kieran.

The River Lee flows through the centre of Cork, Ireland's second city, which stands on an island in the river.

The richly furnished interior of Bantry House, which is the setting for elegant concert evenings and around which visitors may wander at leisure.

The mysterious stone circle of Dromberg, near Glandore in County Cork, was constructed in about 100 BC, much later than most other circles.

The fishing village of Glandore, County Cork, which has recently become popular as a holiday destination.

The remote island of Gougane Barra where St Finbarr lived in solitude before founding his abbey on the Lee. This later grew into Cork City.

The garden island of Garnish, off Glengarriff in County Cork, created earlier this century out of a bare, rocky outcrop by gardening enthusiast, John Bryce.

A charming old house overgrown with creepers, in Banteer, County Cork.

The Blackwater River tumbles over the weir at Fermoy, a town gambled away in a single evening by 18th-century Lord Fermoy.

*The 18th-century Tower
of Shandon in Cork City,
which houses the famous
16th-century Eight Bells
of Shandon.*

A couple from a farm south of Limerick City gather their hay harvest in traditional fashion.

A disused waterwheel in the village of Croom, County Limerick, where the 18th-century Maigue Poets met to write their Gaelic verse.

*A tractor rumbles along
a lane near Glin, a
town on the Shannon,
County Limerick.*

*The overgrown ruins of
Carrigogunnel Castle,
County Limerick.*

A small shrine at Adare, County Limerick. Adare was constructed in the mid-19th century by the Earl of Dunraven, to set an example to other landlords of the perfect Irish village.

The great stone circle at Lough Gur, the most impressive of many prehistoric monuments grouped around the still waters of the lough.

A thatcher at work in Abbeyfeale, County Limerick. The rolling countryside south of the Shannon is typified by thatched cottages.

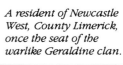

A resident of Newcastle West, County Limerick, once the seat of the warlike Geraldine clan.

A cottage in Adare, County Limerick, a village famed as much for its antique shops as for its landscaped gardens and fine design.

The ruins of the Franciscan friary of Askeaton, County Limerick, founded in 1389 by the Earl of Desmond and designed with great elegance.

Limerick Castle, built by King John in the early 13th century, but remodelled in the late 16th century to with-stand cannons and gunpowder.

The cottages fringing the main street of Adare, County Limerick, a village designed to be visually attractive as well as functional.

THE

SOUTHEAST

A charming, white-washed cottage on the Waterford Road, southeast of Limerick.

The original sign, since replaced, which proclaims the place where births, marriages and deaths for all Tipperary have to be registered.

A forestry road in the Galtee Mountains of southwestern Tipperary.

The Glen of Aherlow in the Galtee Mountains, which features on several hiking trails and has several walkers' hostels nearby.

A dramatic sky seen over Lough Derg from the site known as the Graves of the Leinstermen.

The ruined castle of Dromineer on Lough Derg, which overlooks a fine harbour used by yachts and other pleasure craft.

Lough Derg, a tranquil stretch of water where visitors may hire boats or board one of the regular cruises which visit the small, wooded islands.

A boat rocks gently on the evening ripples of Lough Derg, a lake particularly well-known for its fishing.

The Rock of Cashel,
ancient fortress of the
Kings of Munster, where
St Patrick carried out
several baptisms and a
monastery was founded.

A swan swims elegantly
across the surface of
Lough Derg.

Farm workers making
a traditional hayrick on
water meadows to the
north of Cashel. Such
methods of storing
winter food for the live-
stock have changed little
since the cattle-raiding
of pre-Christian days.

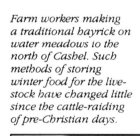

The round tower beside the Bay of Ardmore is of 11th century origin, but this peculiarly Irish form of fortification dates back to around the 7th century.

A waterfall tumbles down a rocky ravine in the bare Monavullagh Mountains of central County Waterford.

An expert craftsman cuts a crystal bowl in the famous crystal works of Waterford.

The furnaces at the Waterford Crystal Glass Factory. The glass-blowing industry began in the 16th century, but crystal was not produced until the close of the 18th century.

A beautifully kept cottage garden in Dunmore East. The single storey, slate-roofed cottage with a small garden is typical of this area.

Boats rest in a small harbour near Tramore, a holiday area popular with families from the southern towns on weekend trips to the seaside.

A boggy hollow in the Monavullagh Mountains, an area popular with hikers who are able to undertake gruelling hikes and withstand the battering of rough weather.

A quiet corner of Passage East, an attractive village high above Waterford Harbour. Characterised by its small whitewashed buildings, and once fortified, it is a place full of interest.

The striking Tholsel in Kilkenny City, which dates back to a 6th-century monastery, which was replaced in the 12th century by a Norman fortified town.

One of the famous, black marble tombs of St Canice's Cathedral in Kilkenny. The church was constructed in the 13th century.

The interior of Kilkenny Castle, built in medieval times and fully restored in the 19th century. The castle outline dominates the city.

St Laserain's Church in
Old Leighlin, which was
once the centre of a
bishopric and still
retains the ruins of a
7th-century monastery.

A colourful wayside
shrine at Myshall in
one of the more rural
sections of County
Carlow.

The bridge over the River
Barrow at Carlow Lock.
The Barrow is one of the
more attractive of
Ireland's rivers for
pleasure cruising.

Hookhead Lighthouse, said to be the oldest in Europe, has records that date back to the 12th century. The surrounding coastal flats are rich in birdlife.

An auction house in Wexford. The city was founded by Vikings in the 9th century and remained an important port until the harbour silted up last century.

A yeoman farmer of County Wexford. The county is a fertile, fruit-growing region which has enjoyed more contact with Europe than most of Ireland.

A thatcher at work using traditional tools on the Ferrycarrig Folk Park, where past ways of life and skills are recreated for tourists.

THE EAST AND

MIDLANDS

The River Liffey flows through Dublin. The capital city of Ireland began as a fortress built by raiding Vikings, but within a generation became the premier port of the island.

The Rock of Dunamase, a prehistoric fortress which was continuously inhabited for centuries, until 1645 when it was stormed by Cromwell and systematically destroyed.

The fertile countryside of County Laois, formerly named Queen's County after Queen Mary I who handed the richer lands to her supporters.

A window box in Portlaoise, a major rail junction which features on many tours of Ireland.

The great cross at Clonmacnoise, erected in the 10th century. The cross commemorates King Flann and Abbot Coman with carved scenes of the monastery's early history.

A sign points the way to Clonmacnoise, a monastery which was both a seat of learning, and the burial place of the Kings of Tara.

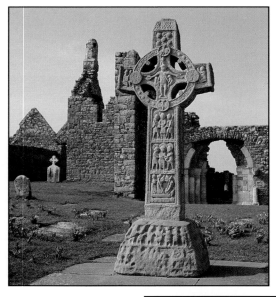

The ruins of the monastery of Clonmacnoise. Founded in 548, the monastery was secure among the Shannon bogs until 1552, when it was looted by English soldiers.

A playful dog wrestles with the painter of one of the many rowing boats available for hire on the Shannon, near Clonmacnoise.

Hough's pub in the village of Banagher, on the banks of the Shannon. It was in a neighbouring house that Anthony Trollope wrote his first works.

County Offaly is traditionally an area of bog, the Bog of Allan and the Boora Bog, which were both long impassable. In the south are extensive woodlands.

Horses graze on the extensive grasslands around Kildare. For centuries the rich grazing lands have been famous for their horses.

The library in the magnificent, 18th-century mansion, Carton House, the ancestral home of the Earls of Kildare.

The Moone High Cross which stands some 17 feet high and has over 50 carved panels. It is thought to date back to the 9th century.

The round tower at
Glendalough Monastery,
which was founded in
the 6th century by St
Kevin, a member of the
Leinster royal family.
The monastery was later
abandoned during
the 16th century.

Glencree Valley, once a
thickly forested region,
but now a fertile valley
beneath the Wicklow
Mountains.

A local leads his dogs
across the shingle
beaches of Wicklow.
Much of the county's
coast is occupied by
suburbs of Dublin.

*A village church near
Rathdrum, set in
territory famous for
its woodlands.*

A typical rural village store with its rough construction and wide range of goods for sale.

The Upper Lake at Glendalough, the valley of the twin lakes. This quiet and isolated valley attracted the hermit St Kevin in the 6th century, when he fled an unwanted marriage.

The falls of Glenmacness near Laragh. This was traditionally lawless country where the hillmen lived by their own codes, which owed little to the kings and earls of the lowlands.

The gushing stream which forms the source of the Inchavore River high in the Wicklow Mountains.

The farms of south-western Wicklow provide the richest pasture land of the county, and are home to large herds of cattle.

Once the Canal Hotel, this fine building is situated on Portobello Canal and Lock.

A colourful flowerstall in a Dublin street. The famous markets of the city are frequented by locals looking for a bargain, as well as by tourists in search of local colour.

Many of the vegetables which pack the market stalls of Dublin are brought in by lorry from the farms of Wicklow, Kildare and Meath.

A piper in traditional, ceremonial costume plays at the Hurling Final in Croke Park, also the site of Gaelic football matches and other sporting events.

Trinity College, Dublin, was founded in 1592 on the site of a 12th-century monastery. Few buildings, however, have survived from before the 18th century.

The interior of Marsh's Library, the oldest library in Ireland, has changed little since it was first built in 1707.

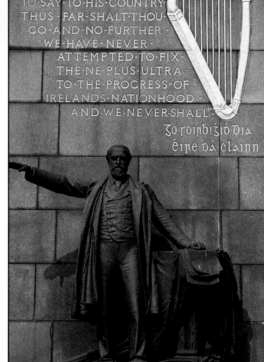

The monument to the great, 19th-century, politican Charles Parnell, who achieved much land reform, but fell from influence due to a scandal.

The vault of St Michan's Church where the limestone walls keep corpses dry, allowing them to survive the centuries.

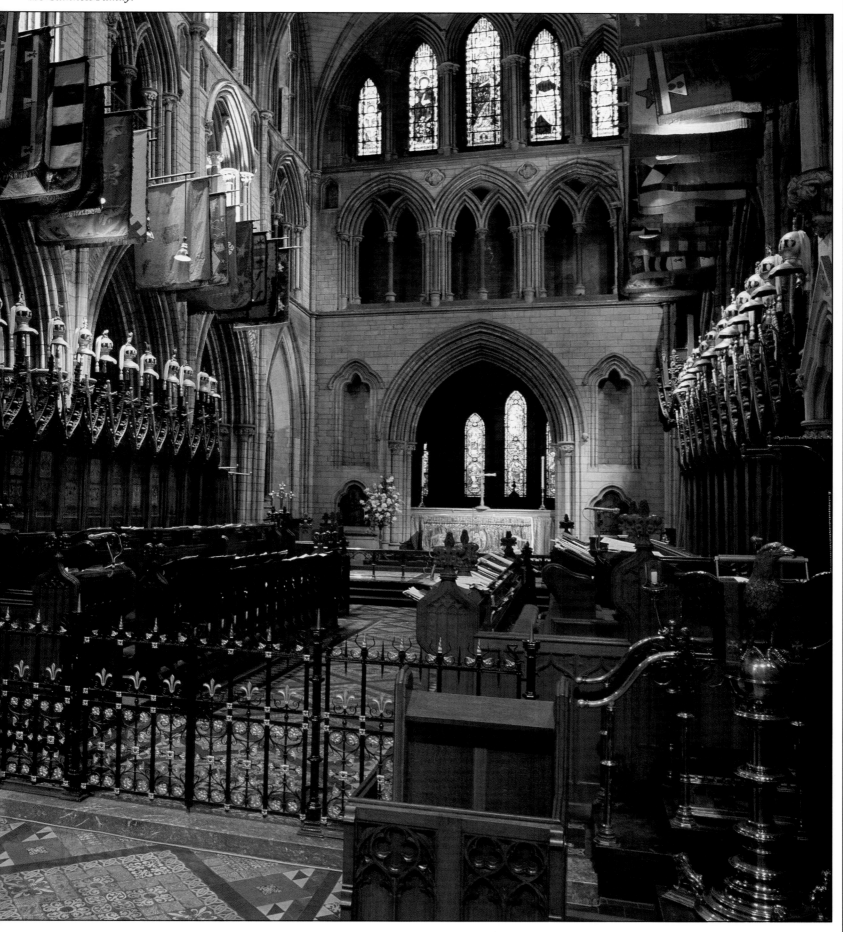

St Patrick's Cathedral, which was begun in 1190, but dates largely from a 19th-century restoration funded by the Guinness Family.

The copper dome of the Four Courts beside the Liffey. The Four Courts were built in 1776, gutted during the Civil War of 1921, and have since been restored.

A small stall in Iveagh Market – one of several cheap markets in Dublin – occupies a magnificent, Victorian covered square.

Merchants' Alley, one of the narrower shopping streets. Dublin, in common with other Viking cities such as York and Waterford, has many such tiny thoroughfares.

The Irish love of music is perpetuated by street musicians and buskers who can be found in Dublin streets at any time of the year.

The traditional prams of Dublin, used for street hawking as much as for transporting babies, are now losing favour to the ubiquitous pushchair.

One of many back streets in Dublin. Although not much publicised to tourists they reveal the atmosphere of Georgian architecture just as much as the grander buildings.

Children sit on Queen Maeve Bridge, which links the shopping and theatrical heart of Dublin north of the Liffey, with the historic centre to the south.

A traditional, 19th-century shopfront survives to lend its period style to an antique shop.

One of the fine door knockers which adorn the elegant facades of the finer Dublin houses.

The staircase in the National Gallery. With over 2,000 works on show the gallery is one of the finest in the city.

Marsh's Library which stands beside St Patrick's Cathedral and contains books which once formed Dean Swift's personal collection.

A pair of magnificent, Georgian doorways near Merrion Square. Dublin is famous for its period architecture and boasts some fine houses.

An exhibit in the National Gallery. George Bernard Shaw left the Gallery one third of his wealth in appreciation of its works.

The Liffey flows past the Four Courts. It was the navigable Liffey which drew the Viking seafarers who founded the city in the 9th century.

Colourful market stalls litter the roadside, offering a wide selection of fresh fruit, vegetables and flowers.

Beachfront near Dublin.

Typical Victorian, domestic chimney pots backed by a modern high rise block. Much of historic Dublin is being swept away by developments.

A charmingly, hand-painted street sign giving the name of a narrow road open only to pedestrians.

The imposing entrance to the Iveagh Market, now the favoured location for second-hand clothes dealers.

The Guinness Brewery where Ireland's favourite beer is produced. The Brewery now runs a guided tour and has a souvenir shop for visitors.

A bridge crosses the Liffey. Dublin's early trading success was based on a ford crossing the river just upstream of the docks, which are capable of taking sea-going ships.

Elegant shops and cafes in the Powerscourt Town House Centre.

Arran Quay – the riverside streets are still known as 'quays,' a reminder of the time when ships tied up on the Liffey to load and unload for international trade.

A quiet stroll over a lock on the Grand Canal, which winds through the city centre and once formed the industrial thoroughfare.

A beautifully ornate interior of one of Dublin's Victorian bars, which has escaped the commercial pressure to redevelop.

An elaborate and original shopfront, complete with mosaic pavement, now converted into a chic restaurant.

The graceful Halfpenny
Bridge, silhouetted at
sunset against the
incomparable backdrop
of Dublin city centre.

The Halfpenny Bridge,
linking Bachelors Walk
and Aston Quay, is open
to pedestrians only.

Tara, the ancient home
of the High Kings of
Ireland. Extensive
earthworks and the
holy stone are all that
remain of the palaces
and feasting halls.

The large, open air
market at Navan, where
the Blackwater River
joins the Boyne and
many routes meet to
form an important
crossroads.

Triple spiral carvings at Newgrange. Although these have been interpreted as sundiscs or symbols of a mother goddess, their real meaning is obscure.

The spectacular entrance to the prehistoric tomb of Newgrange. The tomb was restored in recent years to its original appearance.

The Yellow Steeple of Trim, all that remains of St Mary's Abbey after a visit in 1642 from the fiercely Protestant troops of Cromwell.

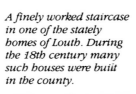

A finely worked staircase in one of the stately homes of Louth. During the 18th century many such houses were built in the county.

Shelling Hill Beach on Dundalk Bay, near the base of the Cooley Peninsula, is an area rich in legendary lore.

Hay bales on the Cooley Peninsula. The fertile land of the peninsula lies around the coastal fringe, as does the only major road.

The interior of the Cooley Peninsula has many heather and gorse-covered hillsides where sheep can be found grazing. It was here that Cuchulainn fought his epic battles against the warriors of Connaught.

Formerly the private reserve of the Pratt family in nearby Cabra, Dunaree Forest Park is now open to the public.

A tombstone in Cavan, the former site of a medieval monastery and now the location of a massive, 20th-century cathedral.

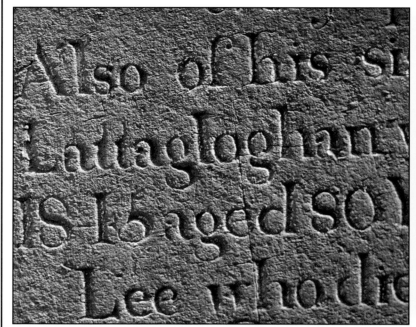

Several well-marked nature trails, bridle ways and walks wind through Dunaree Forest Park, where the native wildlife includes deer and fox.

*A 15th-century,
sculptured corbel on
Drumlane Church. Irish
churches carry a unique
mixture of carved
decorations, including
numerous lewd women
known as sheila-nagigs.*

*Mrs Faris displays
some of her Pighouse
Collection, which she
has gathered at
Cornafean to remind
the public of the Irish
history of pig farming.*

Poor for farming, the bumpy and convoluted layout of County Monaghan is ideal for interesting and unusual golf courses.

The Inner Lake on the Dartry Estate, Rockcorry, a region rich in fish, ideal for walking, and abundantly full of cheap accomodation.

The Inny River flows through open country near Ballymahon, a village in which many people stay when exploring the Inny and upper Shannon valleys.

An old kitchen bucket from Tullynally Castle. In the 1790s this residence, seat of the Earls of Longford, was converted to a romantic castle.

A boat tied up near the shores of Lough Corrib after a day's fishing on the quiet waters.

The massive Church of St Peter and St Paul at Athlone, built for Ireland in the 1930s in the unusual, Italian Renaissance style.

The Market House of Mullingar now houses a folklore museum, which concentrates on the rural life of this popular fishing region.

The restored equipment of the Tullynally Castle kitchens, which now form the basis of the working displays at this post-medieval stately home.

THE WEST

The statue of St Patrick on Croagh Patrick, the rugged mountain where St Patrick fasted and prayed for 40 days and where a modern chapel has since been built.

A blacksmith using traditional tools and techniques to produce implements and equipment in Bunratty Park Folk Museum.

The reconstructed crannog, or Iron Age lake dwelling at Craggaunowen, where other recreated buildings and boats are also on display.

A shop at Bunratty Park Folk Museum, where traditional goods and craftwork are on sale beside the restored Bunratty Castle.

Picturesque shops in Bunratty Park Folk Museum. The castle was restored in the 1950s by Lord Gort, and the folk museum and displays have developed since.

The trout fishing of Clare is famous and many of the people of Clare earn a living from catching fish or providing services for visiting anglers.

One of several cottages in Bunratty Park Folk Museum that were moved here to escape demolition when Shannon Airport was extended.

The dolmen known as Poulabrone, 'the pool of sorrows', on the Burren. The stark stones are the remnants of a pre-historic burial chamber.

The River Cullenagh tumbles through its wooded valley at Ennistymon, a typically colourful Clare village.

The graveyard of Caher Connell near Lisdoon-varna, the spa favoured by courting couples and famed for its radioactive mineral waters.

Taking a rest from work; small farming commu-nities thrive on the islands which dot the Shannon Estuary where it opens out into a large bay.

The Little Ark of Moneen which Catholic villagers wheeled into the shallows of the sea, in order to hold services beyond the legal jurisdiction of the local Protestant landlord.

A stream tumbles down energetically to the Atlantic Ocean at Baltard Bay in western Clare.

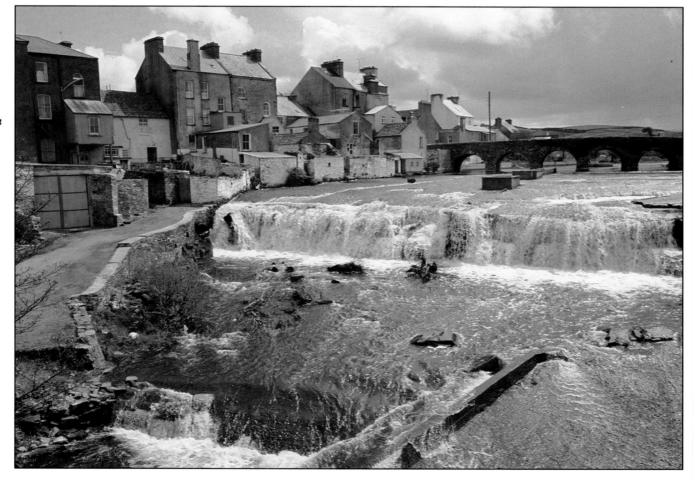

A typically busy street in Galway, the commercial centre for western Ireland, as it has been since the 13th century.

A trader working on the Ballybrit Racecourse during the annual July Galway Races, held just outside Galway City.

A makeshift betting office on the Ballybrit Race-course for the July Galway Races, where the prestige race is the Galway Plate.

A stolid Galway farmer rests in the rugged countryside outside Galway City. The centuries-old animosity between city and county has now gone.

Fishermen bring their boat to moor in Galway Harbour. In September the city hosts the Galway Oyster Festival, which features the International Oyster Shucking Championships.

The still waters of Killary Harbour, a long, narrow finger of sea which reaches inland to the Falls of Aasleagh.

A ruined cottage beside a tumbling stream; much of rural Galway has suffered population decline since the 1840s as famine, and better prospects in the cities, empty the villages.

A carved detail from the doorway of Clomfert Cathedral, a church much smaller than most.

Traditional scything of hay grass on an open field near Roundstone. Even in Galway more modern methods are gaining ground.

Cottages on Inishmaan, the Aran Island less frequently visited by tourists and so more original in style.

An aerial view of Dun Eoghanachta, one of several prehistoric stone fortresses on Inishmore, the largest of the Aran Islands.

The Aran Island inhabitants are staunchly Gaelic speaking, but easily turn to English when visitors arrive. Most islanders spend their youth working in Britain or America.

Horse-powered farm machinery can still be found in western Galway where traditional methods persist.

The roofless Portumna Castle which stands at the heart of the vast, forested estate, formerly belonging to the Earls of Clanrickarde.

The Connemara is the largest Gaelic-speaking area of Ireland and preserves much of the traditional way of life. The Connemara Pony Show enables local youngsters to display their mounts and riding skills.

The fishing harbour at Roundstone, a village at the foot of the Maumturk Mountains which combines tourism and a busy fishing industry.

A tranquil stream flows through a village on Nun's Island.

The bog wilderness around Lake Maumeem with the grand Twelve Bens of Connemara beyond.

A cottage at Leenan at the head of Killary Harbour, a natural arm of the sea which reaches deep into the Galway/Mayo borderlands.

The Bog Garden in the Lough Key Forest Park at Boyle, where bog plants from across Ireland are kept and pampered.

A ruined windmill at Elphin in the predominantly flat landscape of eastern Roscommon, which lies along the Shannon.

Rags left as offerings beside St Lasair's Well at Kilronan. St Lasair is said to have been the daughter of St Ronan, who founded the church, but many folklorists see this as a Christianised, pagan holy well.

St Lasair's Well, near which is buried the last of Ireland's itinerant harpist-bards, Turlough O'Carolan, who died in 1733.

The indented shores
of Lough Conn where
mammoth pike of up
to 53 pounds have been
caught.

A shopfront in Westport,
a town which was laid
out for the Marquess of
Sligo in the 18th century,
by the famous architect
James Wyatt.

*A country road winds
through a typical
Connemara landscape
of bog and mountain.*

The Chancel at Ballintubber Abbey which was founded in the 13th century by Cathal of the Wine Red Hand, King of Connaught, and where Mass is still sung.

A sign at the base of the rugged mountain Croagh Patrick, giving pilgrims instructions on the proper method of pilgrimage.

*The view of scenic Clew
Bay from the summit
of the holy mountain,
Croagh Patrick.*

*The lonely shores of
Westport Bay where
an international sea-
angling championship
is held each summer.*

*The dramatic cliffs
around Achill Head, on
Achill Island, a favourite
tourist destination with
its fine scenery and
enticing beaches.*

The elegant interior of Ashford Castle which, despite its medieval appearance, was built in the 19th century for the Guinness family.

Turning hay above the shores of Lough Conn, one of the largest lakes of northern Mayo and a fine source of fish.

THE

NORTHWEST

A hayrick in a mountain glen near the fishing port of Killybegs.

A flock of sheep moving down a lane in the wooded valley which shelters Glencar and its lakes.

Much used by small-holders, a traditional donkey cart is tied to a wall in Collooney.

A traditionally decorated pub frontage of County Sligo, where many pubs make a feature of local music.

A shop is distinguished from surrounding houses only by the signs which advertise the wares which are on sale.

The dramatic 50-foot-tall waterfall of Glencar, near Manorhamilton, which is especially impressive after heavy rainfall.

The Shannon at Carrick-on-Shannon, which has become a leading touring centre with numerous hotels, including some of the best in the island.

The tiny, village post office of Largydonnell; Gaelic signs are common even beyond the Gaelic-speaking areas.

The dramatic home of Mullaghmore Castle, built in the early 19th century and still maintained as a fine, private home.

A tractor trundles across the Inishowen Peninsula. Once a stronghold of the O'Neill kings of Ulster, the area is now a quiet rural region.

Cattle graze above Lough Swilly, from which the Gaelic Earls of Tyrconnell and Tyrone fled into exile in 1607.

A cattle auction in Donegal, one of the smallest and most rural of the county towns in Ireland.

Sheep graze on the grasslands of the Gap of Mamore on the Inishowen Peninsula, which is surprisingly little visited by foreign tourists.

Milking a cow in the field was the traditional way of milking in Donegal, where cow byres were few and far between.

An overgrown stone wall forms an almost forgotten barrier between upland fields on the Inishowen Peninsula.

A tranquil scene on Mulroy Bay, a sealough dotted with forested islands.

St Patrick's Purgatory on Lough Derg, where each summer pilgrims come to fast for 36 hours, walk barefoot round the stations of the cross, and pray all night without rest.

A seapost marked with the depth of the water to aid sailors navigate the tidal waters.

Sunset over Trawbreaga Bay, near Drumaville.

Small fishing boats rest on the waters of Killybegs Harbour, also the home port of large Atlantic trawlers.

A weatherbeaten fishing smack rests at low tide on the sands off Carrowkeel.

Donegal fishermen are proud of their salmon rivers and stocks of lake trout. Many people earn a living catering for the annual influx of foreign anglers.

Donegal villages make few concessions to commercialism. Only the cigarette advertising reveal this house to be a shop.

A quiet evening pint of Guinness is much appreciated as the reward for a day's work.

THE

NORTHEAST

Scrabo Tower, an early-Victorian monument to the third Marquess of Londonderry. Built of local black volcanic stone, it dominates the scenery southeast of Belfast.

The two Lough Ernes have a long history, with some of the oldest archaelogical remains in Ireland being discovered along their shores.

The forested slopes which tower above Lower Lough Erne, the more scenically attractive of the twin lakes.

A stream in Gortin Glen Forest Park, one of the favourite stopping places on the long distance footpath, the Ulster Way.

An aerial view of the compact and clearly defined Drum Major Forest Park, photographed on an autumn afternoon when the trees are just beginning to turn.

The expansive sandy beaches which stretch for miles around Castlerock, and easy access via the main A2 road, make this village a popular resort.

The rocky heights above Binevenagh provide a fine backdrop to the fertile countryside around the village.

The elegant Mussenden Temple, built as part of the Downhill Estate by wealthy and eccentric Frederick Hervey, Earl of Bristol and Bishop of Derry.

*The Giant's Causeway
which reaches out to sea
from the Antrim coast
as one of the natural
wonders of Europe.*

A peaceful scene in
Antrim, a place heavily
populated with settlers
from Scotland who have
made this area of Ireland
peculiarly their own.

The stately Belfast City
Hall, built in 1896 in
a style to resemble
London's St Paul's
Cathedral, is a prime
landmark visible from
much of the city.

A cottage gateway from
the rural north of
Antrim, much of which
is surprisingly isolated.

A view from Scrabo Hill of the rich farmland stretching between this landmark and Strangford Lough.

A pale sunset over the hills around the Lagan Valley as seen from Scrabo Hill.

*Few surfaced roads
traverse the Mountains
of Mourne, famous for
their grand scenery, but
bridleways and foot-
paths tempt the more
energetic visitor.*

Fertile grasslands
around Dundrum
Bay contrast with the
moor-covered slopes
of the Mountains of
Mourne beyond.

Salmon fishermen
compare flies before
trying their luck on
the rivers of Down.

Gosford Castle, near Markethill, the vast, 19th-century mansion built in the style of a Norman castle.

Lough Neagh, viewed from Oxford Island. The lough is the largest stretch of open water in Ireland, and has long been famous for its eel fisheries.